STUCK ON CACTUS

STUCK ON CACTUS

A Beginning Grower's Guide

David E. Wright

Howell Press
Charlottesville, Virginia

Illustrations by Joe Thibodeau.
Edited and designed by Keri Moser.
Printed and bound in Canada.

Published by:

Howell Press, Inc.
1147 River Road, Suite 2
Charlottesville, Virginia 22901
Telephone (804) 977-4006

Publisher's Cataloging in Publication
(Prepared by Quality Books)

Wright, David E. (David Eugene)
    Stuck on cactus : a beginning grower's guide / David E. Wright

    p. cm.
    Includes bibliographical references and index.
    ISBN: 1-57427-056-7

    1. Cactus. 2. Container gardening. I. Title.

SB438.W75 1996   635.9'3347
PRINTED IN CANADA   QBI96-40667

TABLE OF CONTENTS

Introduction	1
No Brain Strain in This Book	3
In the Beginning	4
Black Plague and Black Thumb Are Different	6
Chopsticks, Bent Forks, and First Aid	7
A Last Will and Testament May Be Included	14
A Formal Introduction Won't Be Necessary	16
Poles, Barrels, Flat Potatoes, and Hangovers	19
Party Time and Then a Nice Siesta for Me	23
Cactus Fritter or Cactuscicle	25
The "Big Secret"	27
Lighting the Way	32
Is That a New Perfume You're Wearing?	36
Taming the Cactus Monsters	38
The Terminators	42
Monsters of the Night	45
The Monsters Are Gone, So Now What Is This?	48
Soap Opera or Just Good Clean Fun?	51
Name That Tune	52

There Is No Such Thing as Being Slightly Potted   54

Soil Your Pots with One of These   57

A Story of Pots and Pot Holes   59

Pit Bulls and Pot Preparations   61

Just Where Did You Dig Up These Words?   63

Standing on Their Own Two Roots   66

Support Your Local Cactus   68

Magic Beans and Cactus Seeds Are Not Related   70

Fact or Fiction?   71

Seek and You Will Find   73

Ask and You Will Receive   77

Index   78

INTRODUCTION

My original intent was to write a few short pages of information about cactus. This was just to make it easier for me to answer questions about how to keep cactus without killing them within the first two months after purchase. I hear some very sad tales about healthy specimens of cactus, which could have been cherished forever, that only last two or three weeks before passing away. This passing almost always seems to leave the grieving owners with the belief that they were born with a killer instinct toward cactus, or that a black thumb must run in their family. When people discover that I have more than one or two cactus in my possession and that those cactus are not just living but doing well enough to actually bloom, their reactions run from doubt to amazement. Some ask what mysterious gods have I been praying to, or if I have connections with some powerful sorcerer who has bestowed me with magic spells.

My two grown daughters asked for a couple of cactus for their homes and directions for their care. I hurriedly scratched out some rough notes, which I thought would cover everything. Several long distance phone calls later, it was obvious that the information I had given them was not enough, and what I had written down was not as clear as I had intended.

Realizing this information was easy for me to understand, but difficult for someone new to cactus, I made a few half-hearted attempts at writing down what I had really meant in the first place. My wife and best friend, Lois, gave me the final push to sit down and get busy when she indicated that I should either fish or cut bait (something like that). Well, here I am fishing.

Lois and my mother Ruby are responsible for my introduction to cactus. This has led to my addiction to sharp spines. Most of my cactus now live in their own little greenhouse, but there was a time when my wife and I shared just about every room in our house with them. The master bedroom was the one exception as a matter of personal safety, should either of us happen to get up and stumble around in the middle of the night.

This book is an accumulation of six years' worth of simple, keep 'em alive information about cactus that I have gathered for my own needs. The public library has been an excellent source of valuable reading material on the subject; some of the books were far beyond the range of plant education that I needed, while a few others were closer to what I was looking for.

I have bent the ear of more than one or two people who have even a passing acquaintance with cactus, asking questions and then more questions. All of them have been patient and very generous with good answers. To each of them I am grateful.

And most of all, a large thanks to my most critical editors, my wife Lois and my daughters Susan and Tamra, and to family and friends who have taken special delight in pointing out my flaws and shortcomings by helping me with the editing. ⚘

NO BRAIN STRAIN IN THIS BOOK

The main reason most people have a hobby is for enjoyment. Here are three good "keepsakes" to help you enjoy cactus or any other hobby. Remember to:

KEEP IT SIMPLE.
KEEP IT INEXPENSIVE.
KEEP IT FUN.

IN THE BEGINNING

STICKER PLANTS WERE NOT ALL CREATED AS CACTUS

The cactus family is native only to the North and South American continents, even though many cactus plants are found growing in Spain and other warmer countries of the world. These cactus have grown so well, in fact, that they have become a problem in some of those countries. These novel plants were introduced into Europe by the early explorers of the Americas. Since their introduction, they have spread from country to country.

Cactus and succulents all fall into the category of succulent plants, though not all are very succulent (full of juices) and some are downright woody. Cactus differ from other plants in that they have very specialized areas on their surfaces called **AREOLES**. The areoles produce the spines, "hair," flowers, baby cactus on some plants (new babies are most often called "pups" or "offsets"), and even leaves on a few kinds of cactus.

Many plants have spines or thorns even though they are not cactus, and some plants in the **EUPHORBIA** (yoo-for-bee-ah) family even resemble cactus. To a person who is unfamiliar with the differences between cactus and other plants that are equipped with sharp, skin-piercing ornaments, this may come as a surprise.

According to *Webster's Third New International Dictionary*, the word *cactus* is used for a single plant, and *cactuses* or *cacti* for more than one plant. Among cactus growers, these three small words have a tendency to be used interchangeably. This can lead to confusion for almost anyone who happens to be listening to a discussion about this unique plant family. I include myself as one of these

4

easily confused people who just want to keep up with the conversation. Rather than worry about a grammatical discussion on the correct use of these words, and to avoid more confusion, I have chosen to use the term **CACTUS** in all cases, whether I am referring to one or more cactus plants.

BLACK PLAGUE AND BLACK THUMB ARE DIFFERENT

The main difference between black plague and black thumb is that black plague is very real and deadly, while black thumb is really just a state of mind reinforced by bad experiences and a lack of good information. Some people will swear that not one single person in their family, for as far back as history is recorded, has been able to grow anything other than mold in the shower. Others will tell you horror stories about how they have entered a room containing only artificial plants and the plants all wilted.

I have heard it stated several times that cactus are some of the hardest plants to keep alive. This is absolutely not true and I will try to put this myth to rest. The information in this book will show you how to have fun, self-confidence, and success with cactus and other plants. You'll be able to hold your head up when the subject of plants is discussed.

Just think of the awe you will inspire at the next meeting of the Royal Order of Black Thumb when you casually mention that you now have living cactus in your home. You may feel so good about being stripped of your charter membership in that group that you might even start your own select club of ex-Black Thumb members.

I'm not saying that you'll be able to make rocks grow after reading this book, but you will be able to confidently keep your cactus alive. 🌵

CHOPSTICKS, BENT FORKS, AND FIRST AID

TOOLS AND EQUIPMENT

PLEASE NOTE: You can enjoy and have plenty of success with your cactus without any of the tools listed below. I have found these tools to be simple, inexpensive, and, best of all, they work great. These tools make puttering with my spiny friends easier and more enjoyable for me. My tape and tweezers get used less than they used to, but my fork, spoons, and chopsticks are still on the active players list. These tools I use for my cactus work equally well on my other small- to medium-size houseplants.

I admit that this little group of tools does look like a list for a scavenger hunt. And yes, your friends or relatives might inquire about your new eating habits, as well as your strange hygienic practices. (The kidding will stop when Santa stuffs cactus tool kits into their Christmas stockings.) But even with the kidding you will have to take, I believe you will be glad to have this odd assortment in your own tool collection:

TWO SPOONS
ONE BENT FORK
ONE OR TWO CHOPSTICKS
ONE OR TWO SHALLOW CAKE PANS
ONE PAIR OF TWEEZERS
ONE NEEDLE
ONE HAND-HELD MAGNIFYING GLASS
ONE ROLL OF TAPE

TWO OR THREE EMPTY SPRAY BOTTLES
ONE CONTAINER OF RUBBING ALCOHOL
SEVERAL COTTON SWABS
A GENTLE TOUCH
**ONE OR TWO SERVINGS OF PATIENCE, BECAUSE
    CACTUS ARE NOT FOR THE PERSON WHO NEEDS
    IMMEDIATE VISUAL GRATIFICATION!**

Most of the items that you will be needing or wanting, other than cactus soil and pots, can be found around your house or apartment. You may also have some luck at a friendly neighbor's home or at a local garage sale. While you are looking around for these tools, don't forget to check these same sources for pots. And if you are lucky you just might find other "treasures" to bring home.

One of the **SPOONS** should be a soup or tablespoon for scooping soil into the pots if you should decide to try your hand at transplanting. The other spoon should be smaller and preferably have a long handle, like an iced tea spoon. This spoon is helpful for sprinkling surface dressings around your cactus without making a mess. If you can't find one with a long handle, a small spoon with a shorter handle will work quite well.

The **FORK** gives you an opportunity to become an instant state-of-the-art metal sculptor. Just bend about 1/4 inch (or a little less) of the tines upward into the shape of an "L" so that the fork resembles a tiny garden rake. That's it! Instant fame for you, but probably no fortune for all of your hard work, study, and superior craftsmanship. This operation can be accomplished by gripping the fork in one hand and a pair of pliers in the other. Clamp the pliers on the ends of the tines and bend them upward until you get the correct angle. If you happen to have a bench vice at your disposal, to clamp the tines of the fork in, the bending operation will be much easier. You may take a little good-natured ribbing from friends about this tool, but it is wonderful for raking and smoothing the surface of the soil in your pot. It is also excellent for getting loose debris from under the cactus without putting your fingers on the endangered species list.

Please **DO NOT** use Grandma's good Sunday silverware for any of these tools; that would more than likely put a strain on family relations. If you don't have any old silverware to bend and play in the dirt with, then you can almost always find old forks and spoons at a yard sale for next to no money at all.

A single **CHOPSTICK** is all that is really needed, but why not have a matched set so that you can have a spare on hand? The pointed end of the chopstick can be used to gently remove most things that may get caught in the spines of your cactus or for picking off pests that get on the body of the plant. The larger end of the chopstick is great for lightly tapping down the soil when you are setting a new plant in your pot. You can probably take home the pair of chopsticks you use the next time you go out for Chinese food, but be sure to ask first or you might be asked not to come back again. This could be a problem if you happen to live in a small town with only one Chinese restaurant.

The **SPRAY BOTTLE** can be just about any kind of pump sprayer as long as it has been washed out thoroughly. This is excellent for misting your cactus with water or for rinsing off dust and dirt that might accumulate.

DO NOT USE A SPRAY BOTTLE THAT PREVIOUSLY HAS BEEN USED FOR WEED KILLER OR A SIMILAR SUBSTANCE.

One clean **CAKE PAN**, 9 x 12 x 2 inches, will be sufficient, but you may find that two pans are more effective if you have more than one or two plants. The pan makes a fine work area to do any potting or transplanting, and it saves you from having to undergo a major cleanup operation once the fun part is finished. The cake pan also is useful for the pan watering method described on page 29. Using this simple pan for your messy plant jobs will have a positive effect on the whole family, since you will probably be doing the fun stuff on the kitchen table where there is always better lighting.

Smaller plastic dishes, the kind used for microwave dinners, can also work quite well for this purpose. A side benefit of using the microwave plastic dishes instead of regular cake pans is that it will help keep you in the good graces of the family chef.

RUBBING ALCOHOL is used to clean any of the tools in your collection after they are used, before going to work on another plant. Using the alcohol helps keep down the risk of passing something unhealthy on to another plant if one of your plants has a problem that you might not be aware of. Alcohol is also useful for pest control. This is a subject I address specifically in "Taming the Cactus Monsters." Don't forget that alcohol is a very good personal disinfectant for wounds acquired while handling cactus.

The **COTTON SWABS** can be used for cleaning dirt, dust, and pests from the plants.

The **MAGNIFYING GLASS** serves a dual function. It can be used to take a close look at your cactus, or a close look at your skin should you happen to have a close encounter of the worst kind with the cactus that you are taking a close look at.

A simple pair of **TWEEZERS** comes in very handy, not just for the obvious use of removing stray spines from your skin. When used gently, they are great for picking out objects that sometimes lodge themselves under the cactus plant or in the spines.

The **NEEDLE** is in the collection for use in conjunction with the magnifying glass and the tweezers to remove unwanted spines from your body. It may occur to you, from time to time, to use the needle to take revenge on the poor cactus for sticking you full of holes. If you should act on this impulse, you will only hurt the plant you chose to care for. Plus, you will quite possibly end up using the magnifying glass, tweezers, and that same needle to make additional repairs to your own body.

You are no doubt asking yourself, why do I need a roll of **TAPE**? This may not be the answer you had in mind, but here is my answer to your question: The adhesive on the tape works wonders should you discover that some very fine spines, which some members of the cactus family keep in their armory, have found their way into your skin. Find the direction from which the spines entered, if you can, then lay the sticky side of a piece of tape over these spines and pull the tape off of your skin in the opposite direction. You may have to repeat this maneuver a few times with a fresh piece of tape, but you will find that it is very effective for getting the spines out of yourself or anyone else. It is to your benefit to use a type of tape that has very good sticking power, such as wide packaging tape. If you don't have the really sticky kind of tape handy, most other types will still work.

Using a **GENTLE TOUCH** usually makes almost anything you are trying to accomplish more pleasant, enjoyable, and successful. With cactus, this gentle approach can also save you from unwanted surprises and pain.

Wounds from cactus spines, like any other type of puncture wound, can become infected easily. Cactus spines are not poisonous, but dirt and other organic materials can collect on the spines of the cactus and be carried into your body when a spine punctures your skin. Be sure that you use the proper first aid to clean and treat any puncture wounds. This can be very important if you have been using poisonous sprays on your plants.

Here are three other helpful items for personal safety that you might want to acquire if you really catch the cactus fever and get into transplanting:

NEWSPAPER PAGES

Use this helpful addition when transplanting, so that neither you nor the cactus gets hurt. Fold one or two pages into a strip, like a head band, and wrap the band around the spiny body of the cactus. Gently twist the ends of the newspaper together, firmly but not too tight, then hold the twisted ends as a handle for maneuvering the cactus into place.

HEAVY GLOVES

Gloves can be used to handle most cactus plants while transplanting, but I have found that some cactus have spines that will seek out human flesh even through very heavy gloves. When this happens it makes it very hard to remove the gloves, which are now skewered to your hands. Should you find yourself in this predicament, use a pair of pliers or large tweezers to remove the imbedded spines and then gently work the glove off of your hand. Having another person operate the pliers can be very helpful, especially if you have spines in both gloves. After removing the spines and gloves be sure to apply first aid to the injured body parts; the injured pride will heal itself in time.

KITCHEN TONGS

This is a useful tool to have when handling the really viciously spined cactus. Make sure the tongs don't have sharp teeth or edges that could damage the plant.

A LAST WILL AND TESTAMENT
MAY BE INCLUDED

DON'T BUY A CACTUS THAT ALREADY HAS PROBLEMS

Health problems in cactus are usually easy to spot. The four main problems to look for before plunking down your money are:

SOFT BODY
BRUISES AND CUTS
PLANT IS NOT FIRMLY ROOTED IN THE SOIL
PESTS

When a cactus has a **SOFT BODY**, like overripe fruit, that usually means it has been overwatered, frozen, or has an advanced case of rot. If the cactus plant has any of these problems, then you are most likely looking at a dead or soon-to-be-dead cactus. The safest way to check for a soft body problem is to use the eraser end of a pencil. Gently push against the body of the cactus to see if it feels mushy. A healthy cactus plant will have a nice firm feel with hardly any give to it.

Visually check the cactus plant as closely as you can to make sure that it is not **BRUISED, CUT**, or otherwise dam-aged. Be just as selective as if you were picking out fresh fruit in the produce section of the grocery store. No sense in starting out with a plant that might die with or without your help.

Pull out your pencil again, this time to make sure that the cactus is **FIRMLY ROOTED** in the soil. Using the eraser end of the pencil, gently push the cactus from side to side. If it visibly moves in the soil or just feels loose, it is a good idea to avoid buying it and look for another one.

PESTS can be a little tougher to check for, so you might want to take a magnifying glass with you when you go shopping for cactus. The following pests seem to favor cactus juice, so look for them before you buy:

APHIDS are very small, fat-bodied, winged insects that come in different shades of green or black. This chubby fellow can fly, but you're most likely to see him while he's getting juiced up or hanging out on a plant's surface. My experience with aphids is that they will only occasionally bother cactus, but the following four pests are the worst offenders.

MEALY BUGS are tiny gray dots that move across the surface of the plant. The adult females may be located in frothy white, sticky clumps where they lay their eggs. Check along the ribbed areas of the cactus and around the base of the spines for these messy campers.

RED SPIDER MITES are even smaller and appear as red-orange specks on the plant's surface.

THRIPS are very skinny, black, flying insects. They are similar to but smaller than the picnic gnats that get into your potato salad.

WHITE FLIES are similar to thrips in size and shape but they are white and more abundant. These insects rise off the plant in a small cloud when their feeding frenzy is disturbed. (Don't worry, they won't attack humans!)

See the section called "Taming the Cactus Monsters" (page 38) for more information on these pests and how to control them if they should happen to visit your cactus plants at home. 🌵

15

A FORMAL INTRODUCTION
WON'T BE NECESSARY

Among non-English speaking countries it is common to give a person's family name first, followed by his or her first name. The names given to cactus and other plants are usually in Latin and follow a similar construction. This method may seem complicated but it is actually an easier way to look up information about your plants. The *genus* (similar to a family name) is what you will use to find out about the proper care and feeding of your cactus.

GENUS (jee-nus) and **SPECIES** (spee-sees) are not words to be afraid of. Just think of genus as you would your last name, like Clark, Spencer, Kennedy, Clinton, or Smith. Our last names tell us who we're related to in the human family, while the genus tells us who is related in the cactus family. The species name is used just like your first name, such as Melissa, Devin, Julia, Carl, or Mary. First names give us individuality in our own family, and a species name does the same for the cactus.

Cactus found in some garden stores will be listed with their genus and species on a little stake stuck in the pot, although most of the stakes will give you only the genus followed by the word "species." This just means that the grower or retailer isn't sure about the species or doesn't figure that the average person will actually be concerned with this detail. Most nurseries are more thorough and accurate in identifying the plants they sell, or at least someone there should be able to supply you with the species name.

My recommendation is that you start with a desert type cactus that comes in a two- to four-inch pot. This is a good size range for starting your collection and it is what you will most likely find in garden stores or nurseries. This size cactus will probably come with a price tag that runs from $.99 to $6.00. Larger specimens are offered for sale, and some of these good-looking cactus will try to get you to take them home with you. Keep in mind that the price tags and the amount of space the plant will require go up with pot size.

The cactus names I recommend below are only given by genus. The density, length, and thickness of the spines that grow on the different species in each genus can vary dramatically; your plant may resemble a full-grown porcupine or be almost as bald as a baby's bottom. The genus, in my list, is followed by the pronunciation of the word and the plant's general shape. Following the pronunciations are the dates that blooms are most likely to appear on each of the named cactus plants. These dates may vary slightly depending upon your location and the prevailing weather conditions. Warm weather will encourage earlier blooms, cool and wet weather may bring later blooms.

The dates I have listed for blooms may seem to cover a wide range of time. The reason for this wide spread of dates is that cactus are quite dependent on the kinds of winter and summer seasons that occur in different parts of the country. I live in the wonderful, green, and wet Pacific Northwest, just east of Portland, Oregon. Weather in this area of the country is more ideal for growing trees, grass, and mushrooms than it is for cactus. I have my own cactus in two 9 x 11-foot greenhouses that are **NOT** kept at the ideal temperature and humidity year round, like those of most professional growers. However, I do get gorgeous blooms on quite a few of my cactus, even without "perfect" conditions.

I discuss a number of different types of cactus throughout the book, but below I have listed the genus types I think are best for starting a collection. Most of the cactus listed here are pretty easy to care for and fairly friendly in terms of staying alive, so I recommend you choose your new friend from among them. ⚘

ECHINOCEREUS (eh-kin-o-seer-ee-us)
Columnar to barrel shaped.
Tends to bloom between late February and mid June.

ECHINOPSIS (eh-kin-op-sis)
Round to barrel shaped.
Tends to bloom between late April and late July.

GYMNOCALYCIUM (jim-no-kal-iss-yuhm)
Round shaped.
Tends to bloom between late January and early
    September.

LOBIVIA (loh-beev-yuh)
Round to barrel shaped.
Tends to bloom between early March and late August.

MAMMILLARIA (mah-mih-lahr-yah)
Round to barrel shaped.
Tends to bloom between early February and mid
    October.

NOTOCACTUS (no-toe-kak-tus)
Columnar to barrel shaped.
Tends to bloom between early May and late September.

POLES, BARRELS, FLAT POTATOES, AND HANGOVERS

CACTUS COME IN FOUR BASIC SHAPES

COLUMNAR (pole shaped)

ROUND (barrel shaped)

FLAT (pressed potato shaped)

HANGING OVER THE SIDE (known as "trailing plants")

COLUMNAR CACTUS, as the name implies, have the general shape of a column or pole. They are not always tall, some are rather short, some are skinny, and others are more on the plump side. You have probably seen a really huge version of this type of cactus. The giant *saguaro* (say-gwar-o) cactus, and sometimes others similar in shape, appear in some Western movies and are often taller than a man on horseback.

NOTE: While searching your local nursery, you may be tempted by the striking "old man" cactus, which has what appears to be white hair all over its body. Old men can be grumpy, with a tendency to be somewhat difficult to keep happy. I recommend that you wait to invite one of these handsome old men into your home until you have a few successes under your belt.

ROUND CACTUS are usually round in shape, just as you might have guessed. Quite often this kind of cactus is barrel shaped and short, or very round and wide. Some of these cactus look like green balls with spiny decorations.

COLUMNAR

FLAT

ROUND

HANGING OVER
THE SIDE

FLAT CACTUS are normally shaped like a round or oblong potato that has been flattened out. Despite their flat round shape, these pads do not make very good frisbees, especially if you happened to be the person catching them.

This type of cactus may be single or connected to similar shapes in large clumps. The individual flat pieces, whether connected or single, are referred to as pads and come apart from each other quite easily. The most easily recognized cactus in this group is the *prickly pear*, another decoration you may have seen in a Western movie or two.

Cactus with flat pads belong to a portion of the cactus family whose genus is *Opuntia* (oh-poon-tee-uh). Very attractive to look at, the *Opuntias* differ from other cactus not only in their shape, but also by producing an extra set of fine spines on their areoles. Some of these cactus have no large spines to show where their "no touch" areas are, just cute little fuzzy patches to invite a friendly pat from the uninitiated. These extra spines on *Opuntias* are called *glochids* (many cactus lovers pronounce this "glah-chids," which sort of rhymes with "gotcha's") and they are always ready to donate dozens of tiny spines to the unwary finger. These nasty spines are hard to see and tough to get out of your skin or clothing, so they are the only reason I don't recommend the *Opuntias* for starting a cactus collection. If you should decide to give these attractive plants a place in your collection then, by all means, read the chapter titled "Chopsticks, Bent Forks, and First Aid."

HANGING OVER THE SIDE CACTUS have thin, flat or long, round branches. This kind of cactus is normally placed in hanging pots or on a stand so the branches can freely trail over the sides of the pot for a better display of their shape and of the very attractive flowers they produce.

A good example of this type of plant is the "Christmas Cactus" with its bright red, pink, or white flowers. The Christmas Cactus is in the genus *Schlumbergera* (Shlum-bur-gur-ah) or *Zygocactus* (Z-eye-go-kak-tus). The two names refer to the same cactus plant that has been reclassified by different cactus experts at different times for different technical reasons. This same type of cactus plant, sold during various seasons of the year, is referred to as Easter Cactus, Thanksgiving Cactus, or a similar name depending on when the plant is likely to flower. They each have only minor apparent physical differences, other than the time of year in which they bloom. The species name for this plant will let you know when your cactus should be blooming.

I don't want to go too far into the growth or care of these cactus because their needs and space requirements are quite different from the slower growing cactus that are the focus of this book. The type of soil that this cactus prefers is more like regular plant soil with a lot of peat moss added to it, similar to the potting material used to grow ferns (for a soil recipe see page 57). These beautiful cactus are native to rain forests, where the temperature and humidity are fairly high and there is little or no direct exposure to the sun. They live in the crotches of trees where decaying leaf material collects, making a perfect environment for the cactus to take root.

The section titled "Seek and You will Find" provides plenty of good books with information about the "Christmas Cactus" types if you should choose to learn more about growing this interesting cactus.

PARTY TIME AND THEN A NICE SIESTA FOR ME

GROWTH AND REST PERIODS

Each type of cactus has its own growth and rest period, similar to the awake and asleep times of human beings, which they need to stay healthy. Other types of plants have their growth and rest periods described as active and dormant seasons. Cactus could be best classified as perennial plants, but since they have no real leaves to shed and be raked up, they just go into a resting state to wait for the coming of more favorable growing conditions. When they

are resting they take in very little water and their individual cells shrink somewhat to protect them from damage due to freezing or other harsh winter conditions. Plant cells that are full of moisture will swell up in cold conditions and burst, usually causing some or all of the plant to die. You can see the same results by putting a bottle of soda pop in the freezer compartment of your refrigerator and letting it freeze.

I have found March 1 to September 1 to be a safe time to use as the **GROWTH PERIOD** and September 1 through February 28 to be a safe span of time for the needed **REST PERIOD**. Your cactus will require slightly different care depending on whether it is in a growth or rest period. I explain these different needs more fully in following chapters. These growth and rest periods should keep your cactus well rested and happy. The actual dates may vary somewhat with the different climates and growing conditions in your part of the country and with the temperature at which you keep your cactus.

NOTE: These rest and growth periods apply only to the *Echinocereus*, *Echinopsis*, *Gymnocalycium*, *Lobivia*, *Mammillaria*, and *Notocactus* previously mentioned. They do not apply to the *Schlumbergera* varieties. *Schlumbergera* are native to tropical areas and have different growth and rest periods from cactus that are native to the more arid regions of the American continents. These differences in growth and rest periods allow them to bloom while other cactus are napping. ψ

CACTUS FRITTER OR CACTUSCICLE

The heating and cooling requirements for cactus aren't a great deal different from our own personal needs. The following temperature ranges are safe for the types of cactus I have listed, and I personally have had great success with my own plants using these temperature ranges. Cactus can survive at temperatures other than those I have given here, but when the thermometer drops below 45°F or climbs much above 85°F or 90°F, then the risk of damage to the plant becomes much greater.

Growth period: Rest period:
70° to 85°F daytime 60° to 70°F daytime
50° to 65°F nighttime 45° to 60°F nighttime

During their growth period, a modest rise in temperature during the day will produce a marked increase in the growth of your cactus. This rise in temperature, to between 70°F and 85°F, will put the cactus juices to work growing spines and body size. Your cactus can be set outside during the daytime if you are having some comfortably warm weather in your area, just be sure to bring it back into the warmth and protection of the house at night.

The 70°F to 85°F range is also good for the production of flowers. If your cactus is in the mood, it just may offer a bouquet of thanks for the attention you lavish upon it.

THE "BIG SECRET"

WATER

So why are cactus so hard to keep and what is the "Big Secret" for keeping them alive? It's really quite simple; it's water. Cactus simply cannot survive if they are watered like other houseplants. Unlike most other houseplants, cactus **DO NOT** like to have their soil and roots kept constantly wet. During the growth period, you should allow the soil in the pot to dry out before adding more water. Cactus with flat pads will require more frequent watering than pole or round shaped cactus.

When you water your cactus during the growth period, be sure to get the soil around the roots completely wet. You can use a chopstick to loosen the soil in the pot down a couple of inches to look for traces of moisture. Use the chopstick carefully to avoid injuring the root system of your cactus. Use watering time as an opportunity to take a close look at your cactus and check on its physical condition.

The rest period is a time when a lot of water is **NOT** required to keep your cactus alive. A drink of water once a month is about all that is necessary to maintain most cactus when they are napping. A complete soaking of the soil is not advisable during the rest period; however, if you notice your cactus is starting to get a few extra wrinkles or seems to be shriveling up, you can water it more frequently.

I use a moisture meter, which sells for between $6.00 to $12.00, to check on the moisture level in my cactus pots. This is a very handy tool for me, but it is not an expense you need to bother with when you are just getting started growing cactus. You can have plenty of success without high technology.

COLD FEET OR A HOT FOOT

Which method you choose to use is up to you but **DO NOT** give cold or hot water to your cactus. They don't like to be surprised by sudden temperature changes any more than you do. **LUKEWARM** tap water is just the right thing to offer your cactus friend. Cactus also benefit from water that has been left to sit in a container for twenty-four hours. This allows the chlorine and other human-added chemicals to evaporate out of it. A one-gallon plastic milk jug, washed out with soap and then rinsed well, is an excellent and convenient storage container for your cactus's water supply.

THE METHODS

The three methods of supplying water to your cactus described here are easy to remember if you think of using your own body in place of your cactus—a kind of "do unto others as you would have them do unto you" situation.

The **PAN WATERING METHOD** is like sitting in a tub bath and getting all of your lower parts wet, but leaving your head dry and up above the water.

The **SPRAY BOTTLE METHOD** is like taking a quick shower in which all of your upper body parts get wetted down and washed clean.

The **TOP WATERING METHOD** (overhead watering) is like stepping under a waterfall. The results are that you will get pretty wet but you will also be a little worse for wear and tear.

AND NOW FOR A NICE RELAXING SOAK IN A PAN

I have found that using a two-inch deep cake pan is the best way of supplying water to small potted plants. Simply set the pot containing the thirsty cactus in the pan, add about one inch of lukewarm water to the pan, and wait. When the surface of the soil in the pot becomes damp, lift the pot out of the pan and let it drain for a few minutes, then return the happy cactus to where it is normally kept. Even if you use a surface dressing in the pot, you should still be able to detect dampness. One thing to watch for when adding water to the pan is that very dry soil in a pot will sometimes cause the pot to float and tip over. To overcome a floating pot, hold the pot down in the water for a few seconds, or until enough water has been absorbed for the pot to settle to the bottom of the pan.

This method is slower than pouring water in the top of the pot, but it has several good points that make it an effective watering technique. The main benefit of using the pan watering method is that the soil in the pot can completely absorb all of the water it needs. This is important after the plant has had a rest period and the soil is very dry. Another reason for watering in this manner is that the surface of the pot is not disturbed by a stream of water poured on it. Newly potted plants benefit from this method because it will not set them adrift in the soil or wash their roots bare.

A KISS OF MORNING DEW

The spray bottle comes in handy when new cactus are setting down their root systems. An occasional misting gives your cactus a special signal: rain is on the way and more roots are needed to collect this rare commodity. Spraying is also a good way to wash away dust, and possibly pests, that may have landed on the surface of the plant. A good spraying every two days during the growth period will keep your cactus quite content. Please don't think this means keeping the cactus continually damp will promote lots of new roots. About the only thing that continual dampness will promote is the growth of mold and other types of fungus.

A TRIP THROUGH NIAGARA FALLS

The top watering (overhead watering) method has some very good points to its credit. First of all, it is easy and speedy. Secondly, if you are watering with a container that is equipped with a sprinkling head, the cactus receives a nice cleaning rinse. For the person who has a large quantity of outside-dwelling cactus to water, this is an efficient way to go. If there are only a few indoor cactus to care for, the pan watering method is better. The overhead watering method is also good for plants in the rest period, when you only want to give the cactus a small drink or add a little water when it starts to look like it is drying out.

LIGHTING THE WAY

Cactus plants come from many different environments. Some normally live high in the mountains, while others grow naturally in places like Death Valley. Each location has a different climate and gets a different view of the sun. I used to have the very mistaken idea that all cactus plants just love as much hot sunshine as they can get. After all, who would even consider that a cactus could get sunburned? Well, now I know what a cactus fritter looks like and I have adjusted my thinking about cactus and the sun.

You might say cactus are just a different kind of people, who have very unusual hairstyles and keep their feet stuck in the ground. The easiest way to understand your cactus, and its ability to withstand the burning rays of the sun, is to think about human skin and the sun. Some people can stand to stay out on the beach all day without suffering, while others need the protection of an umbrella to be able to enjoy a day at the seashore. Other people are so sensitive to the sun that just talking about a walk outside gives them second-degree burns.

"How much light should I give my cactus?" Now this seems like a pretty straightforward question; you're not asking for Grandma's secret Christmas Fruitcake recipe or how much money your neighbor has in his bank account. But the truth is, unless you have a special decoder ring (like the one your nephew sent away thirty cereal box tops plus $5.99 for shipping and handling to get for "free") to decipher the answers you get, you might just as well have asked for this kind of personal information.

I don't know which type of cactus you will be keeping as a pet, or what part of the country you live in, so it is difficult for me to give you completely thorough advice on lighting for your particular cactus. But I have found that the best place to ask about the lighting needs for your newly acquired friend is at the same place you purchased it. Most good garden stores or nurseries will be glad to give you an answer that is easy to understand.

If you are still somewhat in the dark about the lighting needs of your cactus, or if you didn't quite understand what the garden store owner meant by "filtered" or "indirect," then the list below should be helpful.

FULL OR DIRECT SUN

Generally this refers to full exposure to the direct rays of the sun, often during the hottest part of the day. This can last anywhere from a couple of hours to all day, depending on the particular needs of your cactus and the amount of sun that is available to your area of the country. Some types of cactus and young plants are especially susceptible to sunburn if exposed to this type of lighting.

PARTIAL SUN

This can be either morning or afternoon exposure to the direct rays of the sun. The remainder of the day your cactus likes plenty of sunlight, but not a personal view of the fireball in the sky when it is directly overhead. I have found this type of lighting to be the safest and most beneficial to most of my own cactus.

INDIRECT LIGHTING

This refers to giving the cactus the benefit of bright sunlight without exposing it to the direct rays of the sun. This type of lighting comes best through a window that faces

south. To the human body, it would be like sitting on a covered patio where the sunlight can be seen and the warmth enjoyed, but with no chance of sunburn.

FILTERED LIGHTING

This term refers to exposing the cactus to sunlight but having a closely woven netting material, like the kind in sheer window curtains, between the cactus and the sun. This type of exposure allows plenty of the sun's important elements to reach the cactus but not burn it. This is a method very similar to **DIFFUSED LIGHTING**.

DIFFUSED LIGHTING

Usually this refers to placing something like mini blinds between the sun and your cactus. This allows the cactus to receive some direct sunlight, but it gets the benefit of shade as the sun moves across the sky. That way, no one part of the cactus plant is exposed to the burning rays for too long.

ARTIFICIAL LIGHTING

As the name implies, this is not real sunshine. Cactus do benefit somewhat from the light of incandescent light bulbs and from fluorescent tubes, but specialty lights, designed especially for plant growing purposes, provide the different spectrums of light rays needed by all plants to live happy and healthy lives. These special growing lights are the most beneficial for all of your plants that you keep indoors, but not a necessary expense. A point to keep in mind is that Mother Nature never has had to use artificial lighting.

IS THAT A NEW PERFUME YOU'RE WEARING?

FERTILIZERS

Cactus are not big feeders so they do not require large quantities of fertilizer. You can give fertilizer to your cactus at the beginning of the growth period and once a month during the remainder of the growing season. Fertilizers are measured in different number combinations. If you look at a container of fertilizer you will probably see a set of three numbers such as 10-10-10, 5-2-2, or 20-20-20. The first number in the group is the nitrogen percentage, the second number is the phosphorus percentage, and the third number is the potassium percentage. The basic plant needs for these nutrients are: nitrogen for green growth, phosphorus for flower and root development, and potassium for helping the plant resist disease.

For desert type cactus, a liquid fertilizer of 8-7-6, applied at half strength during the growth period, should produce a healthy cactus. There are many good liquid fertilizers on the market and, after using several different types, I found that Stern's Liquid Miracle-Gro®, measured down to half of the recommended strength, gives me very good results with my cactus plants.

Many growers and book authors use a variety of fertilizing materials with plenty of success. Here again, I prefer something that is easy to purchase, fairly inexpensive, easy to store, keeps my cactus healthy, and doesn't smell bad. This last trait is important if you intend to keep your cactus indoors.

When your cactus is in its rest period **DO NOT** give it any fertilizer; you wouldn't want anyone forcing you to eat while you were asleep, and neither does the cactus.

Newly transplanted cactus or seedlings do not need fertilizing for at least the first year. All of the food requirements needed for their growth are in the cactus soil mix. Adding extra fertilizer at this point can damage tender new roots, and quite possibly cause the cactus to die a premature death.

TAMING THE CACTUS MONSTERS

THE LITTLE SAP SUCKERS

A clean environment around your plants and good air circulation helps in the control of these tiny hoards.

APHIDS

These are small, green to black, fat-bodied flying creatures that like to keep filled up with juice from your cactus or other favorite plants. They seem to take delight in feeding on the new tender parts of almost any plant. The cactus's spines offer the aphids protection from their natural enemies, but do not protect the cactus from the aphids.

Green or black aphids are not very hard to see, and are easily eliminated by dabbing them with a cotton swab wetted with rubbing alcohol. If they are partying on your cactus in large numbers, spraying is the best way to crash the party.

MEALY BUGS

With the possible exception of ants at a picnic, mealy bugs have to be the most magical insects you will ever run across. Once they come to visit and decide they like what you have to offer, it will take constant vigilance to make their family members feel unwelcome at your cactus smorgasbord. They appear as tiny gray specks on your cactus and are most likely to be the juveniles, which are about the size of a pinpoint. Even though these tiny magicians don't appear to move very quickly, they will take over your cactus in no time if they are not controlled immediately.

Once the juveniles mature, the females will make themselves a nice nest of what looks like and has the sticky consistency of white cotton candy. The nest material is waxy and resistant to removal. The most certain way to get rid of the mealy bugs is to wet a cotton swab with rubbing alcohol and generously dab each insect and nest you can find. Use the wet swab to remove the nest so that no eggs remain on the cactus. For this treatment to be effective, it should be repeated every four to five days for a month.

If the mealy bugs get out of hand, and the alcohol treatment doesn't do the trick, try using one of the sprays listed in "The Terminators" on page 42.

RED SPIDER MITES

Don't look for fancy webs decorated with dead bugs neatly wrapped in their own little white hammocks like the big garden spiders make to help you control pests. These tiny little guys and gals do not catch and consume their fellow creatures; they are on a strictly vegetarian diet of cactus juice or juice from some of your other favorite plants.

The red spider mite is not a spider, nor is it a true red. It comes in an orange-red color (about the color of rust), and bears a faint resemblance to a spider in body shape when viewed through a microscope. These insects are not called mites without good reason; you really have to look closely or use a magnifying glass to detect them. If you discover that your cactus is being used as an unlicensed health food bar by spider mites, then using one of the sprays I have listed will serve your unwanted tenants an eviction notice.

SCALE INSECTS

Here is another tough guy who is resistant to ordinary pest removal methods. This fellow is well protected by a low, cone shaped shell that fits right down close to the surface of the cactus so that none of the soft parts of its body or legs can be seen. A dab of the cotton swab wetted with alcohol is effective to exterminate the insect, but the shell stays on the plant for you to pick off later. The best method for removing the shells is to gently use a toothpick or your fingernail to remove them. Watch out for the cactus spines when doing this or you may get the chance to use your new tool kit to make repairs on yourself.

THRIPS

These are pesky little black, gnat-like creatures that seem to enjoy cactus and any other plants you may be cultivating. These are fairly easy to control with one of the sprays that I have listed for use in your battle of the bugs.

WHITE FLIES

These nasty little fellows are similar in appearance to the thrip, with two exceptions: They are white in color and they tend to gather in greater numbers. While not a major threat to cactus, they can and will do damage to your other plants. White flies are a bit sloppy in their drinking habits and leave a sticky residue where they have been partying. The mess left in their wake attracts mold and that is not healthy for your cactus. The crowd control method of spraying works well on these little critters.

THE TERMINATORS

SPRAYS

For your safety, care should always be taken when using any sprays for the control of insects. Whenever possible, use one of the non-poison sprays, such as the soap and water or alcohol and water mixes.

The safest and easiest spray to make and use is plain old **SOAP AND WATER**. For the health of your cactus and any other plants that might need this treatment, use a non-detergent liquid soap. This will prevent chemical damage to the cactus. Just put a few drops of liquid soap in a spray bottle, fill the bottle with lukewarm water to the top, shake, and you are ready to go hunting. This very effective method has been used for years and is still a first choice of organic gardeners. Soap-based insect sprays can be purchased at most garden stores, but this is an unnecessary expense. For an easy recipe for soap insecticide, see page 51.

A simple mixture of **50% WATER AND 50% RUBBING ALCOHOL**, applied from your handy spray bottle, is an excellent combination to knock out any of the unwanted visitors previously listed. The nice thing about this mixture is that it not only kills the pests but it won't harm the plants. This mixture also is very helpful for removing the sticky mess left behind on your cactus by visiting insects with sloppy eating habits. Using alcohol saves you from having to worry about poisonous residues left behind in the sprayer, or keeping containers of poison on your premises.

The only disadvantage I know of to spraying the alcohol mixture is that spraying vaporizes the alcohol and makes it more flammable. But if you use this mixture in a well-ventilated area with no open flames nearby (as you should with any spray) then this shouldn't be a problem.

NICOTINE SULFATE is the first choice of many growers who are forced to resort to poison for insect control. If the soap or the alcohol spray isn't getting rid of your insects and you think a stronger fix is needed, then this may be the next step for you. As with any potentially harmful materials, be sure to read the directions and warnings carefully before using the product.

I have found the Ortho® brand product, called Orthene®, is very effective for my spray needs. There are other products on the market that are safe to use on cactus, but this is one I personally know to be safe. It also can be used as a systemic bug killer by applying it to the plant's roots mixed with water. This helps keep the sucking insect problem down because the poison is in the plant just waiting for their first bite. One major drawback to using Orthene® on plants that will be living inside of your house is the odor, which is quite offensive for several days and will endear you to no one.

I stay away from using Malathion® spray, not because it is harmful to the cactus, but because it is not good for some of my other non-cactus plants. The plants I refer to belong to the same family as the Jade plant. This whole family of plants can suffer bad effects from this chemical. I carefully read the directions and cautions on all chemicals that I use and found the manufacturer's warning against using this chemical compound on any plants in the Jade plant family (*Crassulaceae* family, genus *Crassula*). Malathion® is an excellent spray for most plants and would be safe to use on cactus alone, but I have Crassula plants near some of my cactus and don't care to chance getting an over spray or using the wrong bottle.

NOTE: Please remember that nicotine sulfate, Orthene®, and Malathion® are **POISONS**. Handle and use them carefully. Be sure to follow the manufacturer's recommendations to the letter. 🌵

MONSTERS OF THE NIGHT

THE BIG CHEWERS

Keeping the area around your plants neat and clean will help keep your cactus from becoming a midnight snack for these bigger pests.

SLUGS

This very quiet fellow is everybody's favorite surprise dinner guest of the evening. The nice shiny decoration left behind when he comes for a visit is not very attractive to humans. We normally refer to it as a "slime trail." It is this slime that helps him glide right over and around the cactus spines without getting hurt. Although not usually found inside of the house, slugs will do the same kind of damage to cactus that they do to any other plant. You may not be able to see a slug's teeth, but the slug chews large holes in your plants. New growth on any plant is a favorite salad bar item for this slippery creature.

Slug defenses for plants are numerous, so if slugs are a problem in your part of town, try a non-poison method like the one mentioned below before you go for the heavy-duty poisonous stuff. Keeping the area around your plants clean and free from debris is one of the most effective methods of preventing the slug from locating a new dining establishment.

There is a very simple and safe method for catching slugs; the trick is to find leftover beer that has gone stale from last night's party. Place some of this stale brew in a shallow saucer and set it near your cactus. For some unknown reason, slugs like stale beer (maybe the carbonation gives them gas), and if they are in the neighborhood of your plants, they will see who can drink the most and drown while having fun.

Another method using poisoned bait containing **METALDEHYDE** is quite effective and easy to clean up. Place the commercial slug bait on a lettuce leaf (I recommend DEAD LINE®) and place the leaf near your plants. Since slugs feed mostly at night you can discard the leaf and the dead slugs in the morning. Doing this little chore before breakfast is also helpful if you are on a diet and want to cut down your appetite.

REMEMBER THAT MOST SLUG BAITS ARE POISONOUS. BE SURE TO READ AND FOLLOW THE MANUFACTURER'S DIRECTIONS.

MICE

These cute little animals don't seem to let the spines get in their way if they choose to dine on your cactus. As with slugs, mice are more of an outdoor problem but they do come inside from time to time. Here again, you have a wide selection of non-poisonous and poisonous methods to choose from. You may choose to employ a hungry cat for the job. I personally prefer the old-fashioned snap trap method, but each person's needs, humane nature, and hunting techniques are different, so choose your method accordingly.

THE MONSTERS ARE GONE, SO NOW WHAT IS THIS?

THE BIG FUNGUS BULLIES

If you can't locate any crawling, flying, or creeping pests lurking around your plant, but there is still something wrong, then you may have been visited by one of these nasty evildoers.

ROT

Root rot is probably the number one cause of death for cactus that are kept in captivity. This is usually because their soil is kept too wet. Compacted soil is a partner in this problem because it keeps excess water from draining off quickly.

Root rot often goes unnoticed until a cactus that looks like it is doing fine just leans over and dies one day. Other times the cactus seems to dry up for no apparent reason. This leads the owner to the mistaken belief that the cactus needs more water, with the end result being that the cactus continues to dry up, or it goes the other direction and the entire plant rots away as you watch.

The best way to head off the problem of root rot is by loosening the soil occasionally with a chopstick, being careful not to disturb the root system. Also, try not to be too anxious to apply water without first checking the soil for moisture. It is better not to give your cactus water if you are in doubt about its moisture needs than it is to over-water it.

MOLD AND MILDEW

Bruises and unattended cuts on your cactus are open invitations to these two fungus companions. About the only thing you can do for a bruised cactus is cut back on watering it for a short time. This will give the cactus a chance to concentrate its energies on healing and not on new growth.

Powdered sulphur, Captan®, or rooting hormone powder, when applied to fresh cuts, helps prevent mold, mildew, and rot that can follow if the cut is left unattended.

If you should awaken one morning and discover that the evil mildew fairy has waved her black wand in the direction of your cactus, don't give up all hope of reversing the spell. Modern science has unknowingly lent a hand (or foot) in the battle against the evil one.

The magic elixir comes in the form of Tinactin®, Antifungal Liquid Aerosol Spray. This product is sold to cure athlete's foot. You can purchase this product at your local drugstore without having a written prescription from your plant doctor, or a referral from your coach.

I really don't think that a remedy for mildew on cactus was what the research department had in mind when this product was developed, but fungus is fungus, whether it's between your toes or between your spines. This product also comes as a powder aerosol that, when applied as directed, makes your cactus look like it has just taken a quick trip to the North Pole. After subjecting a couple of my own plants to the rigors of a winter storm of white, I worried that the powder coating might be harmful, so I switched to the liquid aerosol and am pleased with the results. (I'm surprised to say that, to date, the Tinactin® folks have not asked me to endorse their product.) Applying the liquid spray to the spot that is affected with mildew every three to four days for two weeks should reverse the evil spell cast upon your cactus.

Keeping debris cleaned up from around your cactus is important in the prevention and spread of these two fungi. Cleaning tools used around the plants with alcohol is another aid in preventing the spread of fungus and disease between plants.

Good air circulation (not hurricane or tornado force) is a must for healthy cactus and healthy people. So unless you like living in a home that is either stuffy as a mine shaft or drafty as an open barn, the two of you will probably get along very well living together. 🌵

SOAP OPERA OR JUST GOOD CLEAN FUN?

SOAP RECIPES

FUNGICIDE
(makes one gallon)

1 gallon fresh water
1 teaspoon baking soda
$^1/_2$ teaspoon Ivory® (nondetergent) dish soap

Mix well and put the mixture in a spray bottle. Spray the entire plant for treatment of mold and mildew.

INSECTICIDE
(makes one gallon)

1 gallon fresh water
$^1/_2$ teaspoon Ivory® (nondetergent) dish soap

Mix well and put the mixture in a spray bottle. Spray the entire plant for the removal of insect pests.

These sprays really work and the recipes are environmentally safe. You can also use the dish soap to clean your pots and tools or to wash up your own lunch dishes.

NAME THAT TUNE

I am not going to suggest that you should pick up your cactus, cradle it lovingly in your arms, and sing it to sleep each night with "Rock-a-Bye-Baby." What I **AM** suggesting is that you tune into a music station on the radio for your cactus or any of your other plants. I can't remember when I've been in a commercial greenhouse where music wasn't played. Articles written about the effects of music on plants, animals, and people all seem to agree that music is beneficial.

Pick the kind of music that you like to listen to yourself and I'm sure you won't hear many complaints from your plants. Excessively loud music or music with heavy percussion (drums) is not recommended. Come to think of it, my body and ears would probably feel abused after being subjected to much of this music. I can't say for certain, but I've heard that heavy metal music will cause plants to grow in deformed shapes and the iron in a person's body to become rusty. (Probably just a vicious rumor!)

Other than music that vibrates your entire house, just about anything you choose will be okay. Different gardeners and plant growers each recommend a particular favorite music that their plants seem to respond to. It is true, their plants all seem to do very well, but it does seem odd to me that these same people tune their car radios to the exact same music, even when their plants are not along for the ride. Could it be that the plants have corrupted these poor people's minds and forced them to tune into music that they wouldn't normally listen to? Or just maybe, the people and the plants like the same kind of music, didn't realize it, and are each content to think that they were the one who influenced the other listener. As long as each party is happy and doing well, what difference will it make to anyone, a hundred years from now, what kind of music is being played?

My own plants are doing quite nicely and, yes, I do play music for them. I like to listen to a wide variety of music styles and I have yet to hear one complaint from the cactus or any of the other plants. I enjoy the music when I am with the plants and I have not noticed any spines or leaves being shed.

Enjoy your cactus, enjoy the music of your choice or that of your cactus, and have fun. ⚘

THERE IS NO SUCH THING AS BEING SLIGHTLY POTTED

Repotting and starting new cactus plants are much easier than you might expect. If you feel like you are ready to tackle the project of potting, there are just a few simple guidelines to follow.

Acquiring cactus soil is very simple. All you need to do is go to a garden store or a store that has a gardening section and purchase a small bag of already prepared **CACTUS SOIL MIX**. Most store bought cactus soil mixes are just fine, although I would personally stick to a good brand name to start with. Your local nursery or garden store can recommend a good brand. The cactus soil mix will probably be sold in fairly small bags, two to five pounds, which will last for quite a while unless you do a lot of transplanting.

If you should get caught up with raising cactus, then that will be the time to start buying soil in larger quantities or mixing your own soil. Just about every book I've read that contains a cactus soil mix recipe has a different way of putting together the ingredients. If you check out library books on cactus that contain recipes for cactus soil mix, you might want to write the recipes down for future reference (just in case you decide to raise a large family of cactus). If you feel like you're ready to start mixing your own soil, I have provided a few of my favorite recipes at the end of this chapter. Feel free to experiment with these to determine what works best for you.

The best time to start new cuttings, repot, or transplant cactus is during their growth period. This growth period varies with each type of cactus, but I have found early March through mid July to be a safe time for potting. The growth period is when your cactus is in its prime for root production and you will be rewarded with more success.

Rest periods are not recommended as a good time to transplant or start new cuttings. New root growth is extremely slow during this time, so the cactus might develop a case of rot, rather than roots. Looking at this from the cactus's point of view, I'm sure I wouldn't do very well if someone were to move me to a new home while I was asleep.

When you have taken a cutting from your own cactus (or maybe the plant just got knocked over and a segment was broken off), or if you were fortunate enough to receive a potting sized piece of plant from a friend, the main thing to remember is to let the cut or break **DRY AND FORM A CALLUS** over the injured area. The drying and callusing process can take from two or three days up to several weeks, depending on the size of the cut and the surrounding climate. For a small, open cut up to about one inch in diameter, one week is about the right amount of drying time required. Always take a close look to be sure that a good callus has formed, though, because humidity in the surrounding air makes a difference in how long it will take the cut to dry.

This drying process goes against everything you've heard about other kinds of plants, which need to have fresh open cuts to take root and grow. But then cactus aren't just ordinary, everyday, run-of-the-mill plants. What I had to find out the hard way (by losing some cactus), is that all I have read and heard about letting the wounded area dry out before planting it in the soil is true.

"Watering the plant in" as soon as it has been set in the soil is another gardening practice that doesn't hold true for cactus plants. Watering the freshly "set in" cactus is a good way to invite rot. **WAIT SEVEN TO TEN DAYS BEFORE WATERING THE NEWLY POTTED CACTUS**. The only moisture that the cactus plant needs to start growing roots of its own is the amount already in the sack of soil mix when it is first opened. The new soil should be just slightly damp to the touch. If it is not, sprinkle a little water into the bag, mix it up with the soil, and let it sit overnight. Having only a limited amount of water available to the root production area of the newly potted cactus forces it to put down new roots in search of water, just as it would in its native soil.

During this seven to ten day adjustment period, use your spray bottle to **LIGHTLY** mist the plant and soil surface every two days, or whenever the surface of the soil appears to be dried out. This will tell your cactus that it is back home in the desert, where a small amount of moisture is all it is going to get from above. This fools the cactus into putting out more roots to pick up any moisture that comes its way.

When it comes time to give your plant a good drink after the seven to ten day adjustment period, use the pan method described in "The Big Secret" (page 29). 🌵

SOIL YOUR POTS WITH ONE OF THESE

RECIPES FOR DESERT TYPE CACTUS SOIL

Each of these recipes fills a one gallon container. Ingredients are available at your local nursery or gardening store.

MIX 1
8 cups potting soil mix
8 cups sharp (contractor's) sand
1 tablespoon bone meal
2 tablespoons dolomite lime

MIX 2 (my favorite)
12 cups cactus soil mix
2 cups potting soil mix
1 cup fine ground volcanic cinder
1 cup coarse ground pumice rock
1 tablespoon bone meal

MIX 3
4 cups potting soil mix
8 cups sharp (contractor's) sand
4 cups compost (leaf mold)

Cactus soils in mixes 1, 2, and 3 should not cling together, dry or wet. When squeezed in your hand, they should crumble apart easily when you open your hand. If your cactus soil mix tends to stick together after you squeeze it then you need to add more sand or pumice to the mix until you get the right texture.

RECIPE FOR CHRISTMAS TYPE CACTUS SOIL

5 cups compost (leaf mold)
5 cups sharp (contractor's) sand
5 cups sphagnum moss (**NOT** peat moss)
1 cup bone meal

A STORY OF POTS AND POT HOLES

When someone mentions pots for planting purposes, any number of shapes and materials might pop into a person's head, and most of them will be okay to use for cactus. The most common containers are plain unglazed red clay, glazed clay, adobe clay, fired ceramic, plastic with attached saucers, and plastic without saucers. Shapes can be round, square, deep, shallow, long, or short, just to name a few. I did not mention metal containers for two reasons. One is that the materials in metal pots can leach into the potting soil when it is moist and damage the cactus (this also applies to plants other than cactus). The second reason is that exposure to moisture tends to make the metal pots really ugly.

I personally prefer the good old standard, unglazed, red clay pots with a good-sized drain hole (1/4 inch to 1/2 inch in diameter) in the bottom. The plain clay pot is porous, which helps let excess moisture evaporate away from the root area. I have also used the other kinds of pots described in the previous paragraph, and the cactus seem to like them equally well. Maybe I should learn to speak "cactusese" so that I can find out what their true preference is. In any case, I'm happy and the cactus are doing very well, so what more should I ask for?

I can't emphasize the point too strongly when I say stay away from containers that **DO NOT** have a drain hole in their bottom. No drain hole means that excess water will not be able to drain away from the plant roots, and they will be more likely to rot, resulting in the loss of the whole cactus. I know from my own experiences that this loss, especially if it happens more than once, will cause a person to become discouraged. Blame for dead plants is quite often placed on one or more of our ancestors for not providing us with a green thumb to go along with the good looks and sense of humor that have been handed down to us.

Don't worry about the cactus soil mix falling through the drain hole. I explain how you keep this from happening in "This Is a Real Crock" on page 63.

To keep from having your cactus (and maybe yourself) removed from the premises, use just about any type of moisture-catching tray, pan, or dish placed underneath the plant container. The moisture catcher keeps water from damaging whatever surface you decide to use as a resting place for your plant. A simple formula to keep in mind is: No water damage to family antique furniture equals no physical harm done to you or your cactus by family members.

PIT BULLS AND POT PREPARATIONS

The most important part of preparing the chosen pot for planting is to make sure that it is clean. It does not have to be shiny and unblemished and it could even look a little scruffy, as long as it is clean and has a good drainage hole in the bottom. To hand wash your pot, scrub it with a good dish soap and rinse thoroughly, adding a little ammonia or an antibacterial type of disinfectant to the rinse water. This is a great way to make sure any disease or mold spores have been removed from the pot. Let the pot dry completely before starting to plant.

The automatic dishwasher is also an excellent way of cleaning any pots you choose. Use only regular automatic dish washing soap, just like doing a load of dinner dishes. Just be sure the old dirt has been scraped away and rinsed out of the pot before it goes in the dishwasher, or you just might provide the lonely "Maytag® repair man" and his Basset hound with something to do. Of course, all of this hard work and worry won't be necessary if you splurge and spend your hard-earned money on a brand new pot.

If you have a special container that you simply must put that spiny little creature into and it has no drain holes, you can do one of three things:

First, you can go out and purchase a drill motor and a rather expensive drill bit made for drilling ceramic tile (if you don't already own one). Since drilling pots can be dangerous, also buy yourself a pair of heavy gloves and some good safety goggles to protect your hands and eyes. After you spend your money and time gathering this equipment, you will be ready to really "do it yourself." I speak from experience about using the goggles and gloves, since I do drill holes in some of the pots that I use, and on more than one occasion have had a pot shatter or break apart. These broken pots keep me supplied with crocking material (which I will discuss in the next chapter), so nothing is wasted and my "Oops, broke another one" is nicely hidden under dirt and rocks.

The second option is to find a willing friend who has the equipment to do the drilling for you. This may be accomplished with a small exchange of service from you. This service could be an offer to mow their golf-course sized yard or wash their four-wheel-drive truck after they come back from a weekend meeting of the local Swamp Rats Club. Dog sitting their family dog (probably a pit bull) while they go on vacation is another service you could offer.

The third choice is to put dried flowers or pencils in your special pot, then find a different one with a drain hole already in it. 🌵

JUST WHERE DID YOU DIG UP
THESE WORDS?

THIS IS A REAL CROCK

By now, you probably have the author pegged as at least moderately unbalanced, and my wife will agree with you. But what is a crocodile doing here amongst the cactus? Well, that's a different kind of crock. The kind of crock I am referring to is a small piece of a broken flower pot (referred to as crockware in England). The broken piece is usually a curved side section. This piece of broken pot (crock or crocking) is placed in the bottom, over the drain hole, of the pot in which you are about to plant your cactus. Crocking material does not have to be a piece of broken flower pot. A broken piece of coffee cup, or something along that line, will work quite well as long as the portion you use is the curved part.

It may seem counterproductive to cover the drain hole, the same one I make such a fuss about having in your pot, but the purpose of the crocking is to keep the hole from becoming plugged by potting soil. Think of the crocking material as serving the same purpose as the strainer in the kitchen sink or bathtub. Both of them let the water get through, but stop the bigger stuff from going down the drain.

A point to keep in mind for your safety is that whatever material you choose for crocking the drain hole, it is a broken piece and will have very sharp edges. **DO NOT USE BROKEN GLASS FOR CROCKING MATERIAL!**

Another very effective and inexpensive (unless you have a whole greenhouse full of cactus to put into pots) material to use is a coffee filter. My wife told me she used these after she heard about them from my mom. After seeing how well they worked for her, and after eating a lot of crow, I gave the filters a good test run on some cactus I was transplanting—with great results. Using this method also helps prevent personal injury from sharp pieces of broken pottery.

ROCKS ON YOUR CROCK

Probably the least expensive, and one of the most important items used to help keep your cactus alive and doing well is coarse, sharp, crushed gravel for drainage. This crushed gravel should be 1/2 to 3/4 inch in diameter and can be purchased where you buy the cactus soil mix. You might have a good supply handy in your yard, depending on which part of the country you live in. Placing this kind of gravel at the bottom of the pot, between the crock piece and the cactus soil, allows excess water to travel from the soil to the drain hole.

River rocks, fish tank rocks, and most other decorative rocks do not make good drainage for the bottom of your pot. These materials are usually smooth surfaced and have a tendency to trap the soil. The soil and smooth rocks pack together to form a seal at the bottom of the pot. This natural seal traps and holds excess water around the cactus roots, which leads to root rot and a dead cactus.

RANCH, BLEU CHEESE, THOUSAND ISLAND, OR MULCH

Top dressing or mulch for the surface of the soil in the pot is an important addition, but not an absolute necessity. Mulch makes caring for your cactus much easier, and it adds a more natural look to the pot surface.

The mulch material used for cactus is different from that used for other plants. Other plants need mulch to stay moist; cactus need special mulch material to keep moisture **AWAY** from the base or neck area to help prevent rot. On the other side of the moisture coin, cactus mulch does help slow the evaporation rate of the needed moisture in the pot, so you will not have to water the cactus as often.

Unlike regular plant mulch of bark dust, sawdust, or other similar materials, cactus mulch is usually composed of rock, volcanic cinder, or other solid substances that don't retain water. This is a good place to use smooth river rock, agate, or other creative and decorative ideas. Sand is not a good choice for mulch; it tends to pack down with water.

My personal preference is red cinder rock or crushed granite. It seems to be complementary to most cactus and allows moisture to pass through easily. I leave this area up to the individual's personal taste. In the past, I have used the pretty white decorative rock for mulch, and it does do the job, but it has a tendency to become dirty quickly and detract from the appearance of the potted cactus. White also tends to reflect the sunlight and warmth away from the root area. This is great if you happen to live in a climate that has lots of hot weather, but the Pacific Northwest is not noted for its warmth and sunshine, so I choose darker colors for mulch. Keeping the root area warm, but not hot, is very important in helping cactus grow well. ψ

STANDING ON THEIR OWN TWO ROOTS

TRANSPLANTING CACTUS THAT HAVE ROOTS

Place a piece of **CROCK** material or coffee filter over the drain hole in the bottom of the pot.

For **DRAINAGE**, cover the crock material or coffee filter with approximately one inch of coarse, sharp gravel.

Gently hold your cactus so the roots dangle down into the pot and the base or neck of the plant is 3/4 inch below the rim of the pot. See page 12 for intructions on how to use newspaper to transport your cactus. If the roots have been very cramped in their old pot, gently massage them with your fingers. This will loosen the roots' grip on the old soil, and they will be able to reestablish themselves in the new soil more quickly. Fill the pot, gently covering the roots, with **CACTUS SOIL MIX** (it helps to have a friend who'll either hold the cactus or pour the soil). When you're finished, make sure the soil and the base of the plant are about 1/2 inch below the rim of the pot. Soil can be added to or removed from the pot to obtain the correct depth. You should leave a little more room between the soil and the edge of the pot (about 3/4 inch) if you plan to add mulch.

Tap the soil in the pot down lightly with the large end of a chopstick, or bump the bottom of the pot **GENTLY** two or three times on the work surface that you are using. Cactus like to have loose soil for their roots to grow in, and they don't want to be firmly compacted in the dirt.

If the cactus you are potting happens to be quite tall, or feels a little unstable when you wiggle it, it will need a little support. Set three Popsicle sticks, pencils, or similar items in the soil to make a tripod over the cactus. The support should be just touching the cactus, without injuring it. This support works quite nicely and can be removed after the roots get a firm hold in the soil.

If you so desire, now you can add **MULCH** or **TOP DRESSING** to the pot. When you are finished, be sure to have 1/2 inch of space between the rim of the pot and the surface of the soil or mulch. This helps keep everything in the pot where you want it.

NO WATERING FOR AT LEAST SEVEN TO TEN DAYS! A very light misting with your spray bottle every two days during this period will help the cactus overcome the shock of moving. After the seven to ten day drought period, you can put this cactus back on the same regular watering schedule as your other established cactus. 🌵

SUPPORT YOUR LOCAL CACTUS

PLANTING CACTUS THAT HAVE NO ROOTS

Place a piece of **CROCK** material or coffee filter in the bottom of the pot, over the drain hole.

For **DRAINAGE,** cover the crock material or coffee filter with approximately one inch of coarse, sharp gravel.

Fill the pot with **CACTUS SOIL MIX** to ³/₄ inch from the rim of the pot.

TAP the soil down lightly.

Set the **UNROOTED** cactus or **CUTTING** into the pot so that just the callused area of the cactus is touching or barely set into the surface of the soil. At this point you will need to support the plant with the tripod described on page 66. Your cactus may need this support for a few weeks or a couple of months depending on how quickly it sets down a good root system. The support can be removed after the roots get a firm hold in the soil and the cactus feels stable. You may notice the new roots running along the surface of the soil. This is normal. Leave the roots alone until they are firmly established, then add more soil to cover the new roots and bring the soil level up to ¹/₂ inch below the rim of the pot.

A VERY LIGHT MISTING of the newly potted cactus with your spray bottle every two days during the first two weeks will help promote new root growth. After seven to ten days you can start watering the cactus using the **PAN WATERING** method.

NO MULCHING until the cactus is firmly established in the pot. Mulch tends to get in the way of the newly forming roots as they search for water and food supplies. ♉

MAGIC BEANS AND CACTUS SEEDS ARE NOT RELATED

STARTING CACTUS FROM SEEDS

Starting new cactus from seed is not as hard as you may think, but it does require more time and attention than you may wish to invest at this point. The process is also a little more complex than what should be covered in a book for beginning cactus owners. If you are interested in starting cactus from seeds, I would strongly advise you to read up on the subject before trying it yourself.

Several of the books listed in the section titled "Seek and You Will Find" (page 73) give excellent, detailed information about the types of cactus that are good to grow from seed and the important steps involved for successful new plant growth. ψ

FACT OR FICTION?

THE UNWRITTEN (UNTIL NOW) RULES OF CACTUS GROWING

I have seen or heard about this list of rules at different times in my life, and each list varied only slightly. I don't know who came up with the original set of rules, but it was obviously done as a lament to life with cactus plants.

We grow our cactus plants following rules like: when to water, how much light to give, what are the best growing conditions, and so on. There are other rules, too—the unwritten rules—and no matter how hard we try to follow the written guidelines for cactus care, these are always there to haunt us:

1. There is always one "easy to grow" cactus that you cannot grow no matter how hard you try or how easy others say it is to grow.
2. If you only have one weed in your potted plant, it will always be in the center of a clump of cactus with very long or hooked spines.
3. Weeds always sprout just before guests arrive.
4. Rot ignores ugly cactus.
5. If a neighbor's cat knocks over one of your cactus plants, it will always be a prize plant.
6. If you chip or crack a pot, it will be your best or favorite one.
7. If you drop a potted cactus, it will always land plant side down.
8. You will run out of the perfect color top dressing just short of filling the pot. The only other color you have will be wrong.

9. When you finally find the perfect pot for a show cactus, the plant will quickly grow out of it or die.
10. Your prize cactus will always be moved by the show committee so that the worst side shows.
11. Flowering cactus always finish blooming the day before the big show.
12. Birds know show-quality cactus and try to help out with their own exterior fertilizer decorations.
13. Cactus with a natural dusty or waxy coating always invite people to touch them.
14. If it rains only once in a month, it will be the day after you water your cactus plants or spray them with insecticide.

SEEK AND YOU WILL FIND

BOOKS

At the library, there are enough books with "Cactus" and "Succulent" in the title to drive you nuts. (I am living proof of this.) Books about cactus can be found under subject headings of *CACTI, CACTUS, CACTI and SUCCULENTS, CACTUS and SUCCULENTS, SUCCULENTS and CACTUS*, and just plain old *SUCCULENT PLANTS*.

An interesting thing I have discovered is that a large portion of the books written on the subject of cactus are written by authors from England and continental Europe. It seems that in the past Americans have taken less of an interest in these unique plants that grow wild in our own country than our overseas neighbors who had to travel thousands of miles to the American continents to see, enjoy, and study them.

The list below includes just a few of the many books I have checked out of the public library. There are tons more, but these particular books are easy to read and have been helpful to me. Most of these listed have good pictures and are not so technical that you lose interest as soon as you open the cover. The list is in alphabetical order and their order has no connection with the degree of helpfulness of each book. I hope this list is helpful.

Cacti and Other Succulents
by R. Ginns; Penguin Books Ltd., 1963.

Cacti and Succulents: A Concise Guide in Color
by Rudolf Šubik; Spring Books, 1972.

Cacti and Succulents
by Philip Perl; Time-Life Books, Inc., 1978.

Cactus and Succulents
by Sunset Books; Sunset Publishing Corporation, 1991.

Cactus: The All-American Plant
by Anita Holmes; Four Winds Press, 1982.

Colorful Cacti of the American Deserts
by Edgar and Bryan Lamb; Blandford Press Limited, 1974.

Flowering Cacti: A Color Guide
by G. Rayzer; Hippocrene Books, Inc., 1984.

Guide to Cacti and Succulents
by Mariella Pizzeti; Simon & Schuster, Inc., 1985.

Pocket Encyclopaedia of Cacti in Colour
by Edgar and Bryan Lamb; Blandford Press Limited, 1981.

Popular Exotic Cacti in Color
by Edgar and Bryan Lamb; Collier Books, 1976.

The Cactus Handbook
by Erik Haustein; Chartwell Books, 1988.

The Complete Handbook of Cactus and Succulents
by Clive Innes; Van Nostrand Reinhold, Co., 1977.

The Illustrated Encyclopedia of Succulents
by Gordon Rowley; Salamander Books, 1978.

The Prickly Plant Book
by Sue Tarsky; Walker Books, Ltd., 1980.

The Punctured Thumb: Or Cactus and Other Succulents
by George Ashley; 101 Productions, 1977.

The World of Cacti
by Danny Schuster; Facts on File, Inc., 1990.

The World of Cactus and Succulents
by Ortho Books; Ortho Books, 1977.

I strongly recommend George Ashley's *The Punctured Thumb*. I went through a number of books on cactus before this one popped into my view at a garage sale. The book is written with the down-to-earth words and humor of someone who has had successes with succulent plants, but is willing to share his failures as well. His book lets the new succulent plant collector feel good about having fun on his or her new adventure.

ASK AND YOU WILL RECEIVE

ORGANIZATIONS

If your interest goes beyond just having one or two cactus in your house, or if you still can't find the answers to your questions about cactus, then an organization like those listed below should be able to help.

THE CACTUS AND SUCCULENT SOCIETY OF AMERICA (CSSA)
Box 35034
Des Moines, IA 50315-0301

Your local library should have a listing for the state branch of the CSSA, which will be the name of your state, followed by the words Cactus and Succulent Society. An example would be Oregon Cactus and Succulent Society (OCSS), where I currently serve as librarian. Quite often the state organization's newsletter, along with its address, will be listed somewhere in the references to cactus or succulent plants.

Not all local cactus and succulent groups are named for their state. The phone book in your area may have the local organizations listed as well as the state and national. If you are still unable to locate a branch of the local cactus and succulent society, check with some of the nurseries or garden stores near you that have cactus for sale and they should be able to point you in the right direction.

INDEX

alcohol (rubbing) 8, 10,
    39, 40, 42–43, 50
aphids   15, 38–39
areoles   4
artificial lighting   35
blooms (flowers)   17,
    18, 26
books   73–76
buying cactus   14–22
cake pan   7, 10, 29–30
Captan®   49
chopstick   7, 9, 28, 48, 66
Christmas cactus   22,
    24, 58
coffee filter   63–64
cotton swabs   8, 39, 40
Crassula   43–44
Crassulaceae   43
crocking material   63–64,
    66, 68
cuttings   55, 68
Dead Line®   46
diffused lighting   35
direct (full) sun   33
drainage   61, 63, 64–65,
    66, 68
Easter cactus   22
Echinocereus   18, 24
Echinopsis   18, 24
Euphorbia   4
fertilizer   36–37

filtered lighting   35
first aid   10, 12
fork   7, 8–9
full (direct) sun   33
fungicide   49, 51
fungus   30, 48–50
glochids   21
gloves   12–13
growth period   23–24, 25,
    26, 27, 28, 30, 36, 54
Gymnocalycium   18, 24
health problems
    in cactus   14–15
indirect lighting   33–35
insects (see pests)
Jade plant   43
kitchen tongs   13
lighting   32–35
    artificial   35
    diffused   35
    filtered   35
    full or direct sun   33
    indirect   33–35
    partial sun   33
Lobivia   18, 24
magnifying glass   7,
    10–11, 15
Malathion®   43
Mammillaria   18, 24
mealy bugs   15, 39
Metaldehyde®   46

mice 46
mildew 49–50
Miracle Gro® 36
moisture meter 28
mold 30, 49–50
mulch (top dressing) 29,
    64–65, 67, 68
music 52–53
needle 7, 11
newspaper pages 12
nicotine sulfate 43–44
nitrogen 36
Notocactus 18, 24
"old man" cactus 19
Opuntia 21
organizations 77
Orthene® 43
partial sun 33
pests 15, 38–41
    aphids 15, 38–39
    control of 38–47
    mealy bugs 15, 39
    mice 46
    red spider mites 15,
        39–40
    scale insects 40
    slugs 45–46
    thrips 15, 40
    white flies 15, 40
phosphorous 36
potassium 36
pots 59–62, 63
powdered sulphur 49
prickly pear 21

red spider mites 15,
    39–40
rest period 23–24,
    25, 28, 31, 37, 55
rooting hormone
    powder 49
rot 48, 49, 56, 59, 64, 65
saguaro 19
scale insects 40
Schlumbergera
    (Zygocactus) 22, 24
seeds, starting cactus
    from 70
shapes of cactus
    columnar 19, 20
    flat 19, 20, 21
    hanging over the
        side 19, 20, 21–22
    round 19, 20
slugs 45–46
soil 37, 54, 56, 57, 58, 60,
    66, 68
spoon 7, 8
spray bottle 8, 9, 29, 30,
    42, 51, 56, 67, 68
sprays 42–44, 49, 51
    soap 42, 51
    alcohol 42–43
    nicotine sulfate
        43–44
    recipes for 51
    Tinactin® Antifungal
        Liquid 49
support tripod 66–67, 68

tape   7, 11–12
temperatures   25–26, 28
Thanksgiving cactus   22
thrips   15, 40
Tinactin® Antifungal
   Liquid Spray   49
tools for working with
   cactus   7–13
top dressing (mulch)   29,
   64–65, 67, 68
transplanting   54–69
tweezers   7, 11

Unwritten Rules of
   Cactus   71–72
watering   27–31, 48, 49,
   55–56, 67, 68
   pan   29–30, 68
   top (overhead)   29, 30
   with a spray bottle   29,
      30, 56, 67, 68
white flies   15, 40
Zygocactus (Schlum-
   bergera)   22, 24

Notes to Stick With

Notes to Stick With

Notes to Stick With

Notes to Stick With

Notes to Stick With

Notes to Stick With

Notes to Stick With

Notes to Stick With

Notes to Stick With

Notes to Stick With